T0329210

CANTEENS IN
THE BRITISH ARMY

MAJOR HARRY CRAUFURD

SURGEON-CAPTAIN
HERBERT RAMSAY

MAJOR, THE HON.
LIONEL FORTESCUE

A SHORT ACCOUNT OF
CANTEENS IN
THE BRITISH ARMY

by

JOHN FORTESCUE, LL.D., D.Litt.

Author of
A History of the British Army
&c.

CAMBRIDGE
AT THE UNIVERSITY PRESS
1928

CAMBRIDGE
UNIVERSITY PRESS

University Printing House, Cambridge CB2 8BS, United Kingdom

Cambridge University Press is part of the University of Cambridge.

It furthers the University's mission by disseminating knowledge in the pursuit of
education, learning and research at the highest international levels of excellence.

www.cambridge.org
Information on this title: www.cambridge.org/9781107585713

© Cambridge University Press 1928

First published 1928
First paperback edition 2015

A catalogue record for this publication is available from the British Library

ISBN 978-1-107-58571-3 Paperback

To the Memory of

HARRY JAMES CRAUFURD
GRENADIER GUARDS

LIONEL HENRY DUDLEY FORTESCUE
17TH LANCERS

HERBERT MURRAY RAMSAY
SCOTS GUARDS

PREFATORY NOTE

A principal difficulty in the writing of this little book has been the constant recurrence of long and cumbrous titles. In the first place the lawful name of a Canteen is a "Regimental Institute." The two are one and the same thing; but for brevity I have throughout used the old word Canteen. Next there is the Canteen and Mess Co-operative Society. I have as a rule forborne to designate it by initials, so far as possible, but have frequently called it the Canteen and Mess Society, omitting the word "Co-operative" for convenience. The Expeditionary Force Canteen is so well known by its initials that I have not hesitated to call it throughout the E.F.C. The Board of Control of Regimental Institutes was mercifully short-lived, as was also the Army Canteen Committee; and I have been able to elude much mention of the Navy and Army Canteen Board. The Navy, Army and Air Force Institute has long since been best known as the N.A.A.F.I. and I have not hesitated to speak of it by these initials.

CONTENTS

CONTENTS

CONTENTS

xi

CONTENTS

PLATES

A SHORT ACCOUNT OF CANTEENS
IN THE BRITISH ARMY

PRIMITIVE armies live by plunder, a system
which necessarily leads to much waste, wanton
destruction and oppression. The organising of
plunder into a system of supply by the chiefs of
an army is a matter which concerns the history
of the Army Service Corps. But the work of these
chiefs was always supplemented by the enterprise
of private adventurers who followed an army with
foodstuffs for sale; and in fact these adventurers
were so essential to the subsistence of an army in
the field that very soon they also were placed under
military regulation. Our own regiments—and
indeed those of all Europe—were originally formed
on the model of the mercenary bands, Italian,
Swiss and German, which came into being in the
fifteenth century, and were the first professional
soldiers of modern times. We seem to have taken
the Germans chiefly as our pattern; and happily
we have some information as to their method of
dealing with these private adventurers or, to give
them their English name, sutlers. The word sutler,
by the way, was borrowed from the Dutch, and

signified one who drove a mean and petty trade; so that the business evidently was not at first of the most exalted kind.

THE SUTLERS OF EARLY TIMES

The sutlers in a German regiment were placed under the control of the Provost Marshal, the official charged with the maintenance of the regiment's internal discipline[1]; and to this sufficiently onerous duty was added that of the regulation of the markets. Whenever, therefore, a regiment halted for any time in one place, the Provost Marshal selected the site for a market, erected a gallows there as the symbol of his office, and fixed the tariff of prices. This last was an extremely delicate duty for, if he made the prices too high, he offended the men, and, if too low, he alienated the sutlers upon whom the nourishment of the regiment depended. For his consolation he had his perquisites—a fee for every beast slaughtered and for every cask broached—though even so he appears to have been none too well paid[2]. Here we

[1] A German regiment varied greatly in strength, but might number as many as four thousand men.

[2] It may as well be stated here once for all that, until the nineteenth century, officials of all kinds in all branches of administration depended for emolument principally on fees. The reason was that, until the introduction of the credit system and of cheques, salaries were not regularly paid.

have the germ of the later canteen, both wet and dry, with the Provost Marshal for Canteen-Steward.

THE SUTLER IN THE EIGHTEENTH CENTURY

The present British Army was made, it may be said, in 1645; and at that time the Commissary provided the men with bread and cheese; though during the Civil War men must frequently have had the opportunity (if they had the money) to buy meat and vegetables in the market for themselves. But when Marlborough entered upon his great campaigns in Flanders in 1702, bread only was issued by the Commissary, and for all other matters the troops were dependent on sutlers who were regularly licensed. Each regiment had one grand sutler, and each troop or company one petty sutler, who received ıorage for their horses from the Commissary; the numbers being limited to fourteen horses for a battalion of foot, twelve for a regiment of dragoons and fifteen to a regiment of horse. The major[1], as the staff-officer of the regiment, was responsible that the sutlers sold by fair weight and measure, and that their goods were sound and wholesome; but it does not appear that he fixed the price.

It was ordered that the men should mess regularly, and that they should have bacon or "other

[1] The adjutant was originally the major's adjutant or assistant. In France he is still called aide-major.

3

flesh meat" twice a week, the expense of which was met by stoppage from their pay. For vegetables, parties were sent out to gather roots, though no doubt the sutlers sometimes offered something better. Commanding officers were further required to encourage butchers (who were likewise licensed) to follow their regiments with a good stock of meat and cattle "on the hoof," and to sell meat to the men lest they should expend too much of their money in drink. This suggests that the sutler's was in the main a "wet" canteen; but it is very probable that the sutler frequently acted also as butcher. It is significant that the day always ended with the call "tap to," which we now call tattoo, signifying that no more drink was to be sold.

A GREAT SUTLERESS

By a strange chance there exists a biography of a sutleress of Marlborough's time. She was an Irishwoman whose sweetheart on an unlucky day got lamentably drunk, and woke up to find himself in Flanders with the Queen's shilling in his hand, an enlisted private of infantry. To join him she enlisted in the Scots Greys, fought in several actions and was twice wounded before her sex was discovered. Now it seems to have been a common practice for an old soldier to turn sutler. We find in Shakespeare's *Henry V* that Ancient (Ensign)

4

Pistol forswore soldiering for this more lucrative calling—

I shall sutler be
Unto the camp, and profits shall accrue.

So Mrs Christian Ross (for that was her name) became a sutleress with great success, having at length found and married her sweetheart; and she followed him with a bottle of beer all through the battle of Malplaquet until, missing him, she found his body among a heap of dead.

From her account of herself (the writing of which is ascribed to Daniel Defoe) she catered as much for officers as for men and, after a long march, would have a dinner ready prepared for a general and his staff. She was, by her own confession, a shameless thief of pigs, poultry, and such like, which would have brought her to the gallows if she had been caught, for Marlborough was as strict against plundering as Wellington. But probably she was not unique among sutlers in this respect. For the rest she was a regular virago who had a terrific command of language and did her "chucking out" for herself. Mrs Christian Ross, or Kit Ross, as she was generally called, was perhaps the best known character in the Army except Marlborough himself, and, when finally she died, many years later, she was buried with military honours in the churchyard of St Margaret's, Westminster.

THE SOLDIER AT HOME

It does not appear that there were any sutlers or canteens in Britain in time of peace, for the sufficient reason that until the very end of the eighteenth century there were no barracks. There were a few fortresses such as the Tower of London, which were used as barracks, but for the most part the Army was billeted in ale-houses, whose landlords were required under the Mutiny Act to provide them at a fixed tariff per man with food, fire and candle. The regiments were so much scattered —the six troops of a regiment of dragoons were often distributed among as many little market towns—that there can have been no opening for a sutler. In Ireland, on the other hand, there were barracks, small and widely dispersed, so that the soldiers might do duty as police; and there it is possible that some old soldier may have been allowed to open a booth for the sale of liquor. Such an indulgence would have lain at the discretion of the commanding officer.

Under the old system, which was not totally abolished until 1871, regiments were the property of their colonels, and troops and companies of their captains, all of whom enjoyed considerable independence. The Army, in fact, was not an army at all, but a collection of regiments. The welfare of the men depended entirely upon the regimental officers, and we shall presently see that all the improvements in their condition have been originated by regimental officers.

THE SOLDIER ABROAD

There were foreign garrisons in America and the West Indies in the seventeenth century, but, beyond the fact of their existence, it is difficult to discover much about them. At the Peace of Utrecht in 1714 we acquired further territory in America, besides Gibraltar and Minorca in the Mediterranean, and these new possessions were a terrible puzzle to our administrators in England. They required garrisons, and, therefore, troops must be quartered in them; but it was a revelation to the British Parliament that Gibraltar, Minorca and Nova Scotia contained no ale-houses, and that consequently something exceptional must there be done both for the housing and the feeding of the troops.

A full generation passed away before the new conditions were fairly met; and meanwhile the British soldier had a sorry time. He did not take kindly to foreign service at first, and no wonder, for he had to undergo much hardship without the excitement of active service and, so far as he could see, for no particular reason. On foreign stations he was fed practically as he would have been at sea, on salt provisions, with, however, generally bread in lieu of biscuit, and with some proportion

7

of vegetables to avert scurvy. Information upon such points is extremely difficult to find; but, to judge from the records of later times, the men were encouraged, wherever it was possible—as for instance in the Mediterranean garrisons—to cultivate gardens and grow vegetables for themselves.

THE TEMPTATIONS TO DRINK

On the whole the soldier of the first three quarters of the eighteenth century was probably as well off, except in the matter of occupation, as he would have been if he had not enlisted. He was drawn from the class of the agricultural labourer. He was probably not more overcrowded than he would have been in a cottage; his food was of much the same quality and quantity—two meals a day, with occasional fresh meat—and, if he had to pay for both food and clothing by daily stoppage from his pay, he would equally have had to pay for them as a free labourer. In temperate stations also he was often employed in making roads and the like, for which he received extra pay. But in hot climates—India and the West Indies— when once the morning parade was over, the men had little to do but to sit and look at each other.

The result naturally was that they drank to pass the time. In India there was arrack, and in the West Indies there was rum, and new rum, which is poison. Not that the vice of drinking was confined to the soldier. It pervaded all classes from the highest to the lowest. But in the tropics many causes conspired to drive the soldier to drink. In the first place liquor was cheap; in the second he was fed on monotonous salt food; in the third, he was mewed up in close low stuffy rooms, often unhealthily situated and swarming with mosquitos, which drove him mad; in the fourth, after his solid meal at noon he often felt a craving for supper and could think of no substitute for it but rum; in the fifth, he was rarely able to read, and reading matter was not too plentiful in the West Indies even when the writer knew them forty years ago.

Moreover, notwithstanding the best intentions, their officers could do little for them. They likewise were oppressed by the heat, listless and bored, with every temptation to idle away their time in the planters' houses, where they were welcome and where liquid refreshment could always be found; and it was very difficult for them to provide amusement or occupation for their men. Lastly, it was almost certain that, during the summer months, yellow fever would come and sweep away the best part of the garrison, both officers and men. Even a century ago the average life of a battalion in the West Indies did not last more than two years; and there were many battalions there quartered, for the West Indies were our richest possessions.

THE SACREDNESS OF THE REGIMENT

These details are given to show how great were the initial difficulties in improving the lot of the soldier; and it must be added that little encouragement was given to him by the country to improve himself. He could be flogged almost to death if he misbehaved, but there were no good-conduct badges, bringing extra pay for exemplary behaviour. Nor was anything done for the soldiers' wives and children who followed them all over the world. Six wives to every company, selected by lot, was the number allowed by regulation to accompany a regiment upon foreign service; and there were agonising scenes when the lots were drawn and numbers of poor women found themselves condemned to part with their husbands, and to support their families at home as best they could. Many contrived to rejoin the regiment wherever it might be, by some mysterious means. The poor creatures were literally lost without it.

It must be remembered that the soldier was enlisted for life, and that his regiment was his home. His attachment to his regiment was deep and touching. In a hurricane at Dominica in 1806 the sentry over the colours of the 2nd D.C.L.I., though repeatedly warned of his danger, stood by them until the barracks were blown down over his head and he was buried in the ruins. Thus even in the West Indies good regimental officers kept their battalions together by some means. There were of course bad regiments and good regiments, much depending on the commanding officer; but generally speaking the officers took care of their men and contrived somehow to make their lives tolerable—to do, in fact, something of the work for them that was later done by regimental institutes. Those who chanced to be wealthy did much; those who were poor (and they were the majority) did what they could.

THE CAMPAIGNS OF THE EIGHTEENTH CENTURY

The eighteenth century was one of continual fighting in all parts of the world—the fighting that built up the British Empire. In India it was done with a fair amount of comfort, every Indian expedition being encumbered with a vast crowd of followers, in the proportion of about ten followers to every combatant. The oriental is a keen business man, and the swarms of native sutlers who followed the line of march served to provide the British regiments with travelling canteens. An army in the plains of India was in fact a moving city. That which captured Seringapatam in 1799 advanced over one hundred miles in a hollow square, with a front of three miles and a depth of seven, within which were some two hundred thousand bullocks, to say nothing of elephants, camels, horses and asses. That army, therefore, should have wanted for nothing.

In Flanders, where there was a succession of campaigns from 1743 to 1747, we find the Army depending mainly upon sutlers as in Marlborough's time, though there was now a regulation—perhaps dictated by the recollection of Mrs Christian Ross's career—that no soldier or soldier's wife should be licensed as a sutler. But in the wild districts of America and Canada there can have been few men with the capital and the courage to follow armies in the hope of profit, while the difficulties of transport were enormous. We have unfortunately no information upon the point, but it is possible that sutlers of some kind received a subsidy from the commander-in-chief in order to make the hardships of these campaigns more tolerable to the men.

The American War of Independence must have been particularly trying to the troops. It was one of the most difficult and least satisfactory of campaigns, a contest against a civilised people in a country of vast extent and for the most part in a wild state. The sphere of operations ran from Maine in the north to Georgia in the south, a distance of some twelve hundred miles; and there were few points in this immense tract which were not touched by a British expedition at one time or another, through the landing of troops on the sea-board. In such circumstances the difficulty of giving the men, whether through sutlers or some other means, anything more than their rations, must have been almost insuperable; and in wars of this description soldiers particularly need extra comforts. There is little, in a primitive country, to be gathered in the way of plunder, and, while there is no glory to be reaped from any success, every reverse is a humiliation. Both sides in fact heartily hated the whole struggle; and it was said, not without a strong leaven of truth, that at the end the contending armies were made up chiefly of each other's deserters. These few words must be said of the American rebellion because, more than a century later, we shall see that a war of the same kind brought about a new era in the provision for troops in the field.

THE WARS OF THE FRENCH REVOLUTION AND EMPIRE

The eighteenth century ended with the long war of the French Revolution and Empire, which began in 1793 and closed at Waterloo in 1815. The first of its important campaigns were fought on the familiar ground of Flanders, where we cannot doubt that sutlers were forthcoming, and were regulated according to the time-honoured system. After 1794 there was little fighting outside the West Indies until 1799, when some thirty thousand men were sent on an expedition to North Holland. The operations lasted little more than two months, and we know for certain that the Army was much embarrassed because it was joined by no sutlers. The troops in fact had nothing but water to drink, for they were entirely dependent on sutlers for spirits.

The next serious campaigns were those in the Peninsula from 1808 to 1814. They were in one way a new departure. Hitherto the British had always conducted what may be called their "big" wars in the Low Countries, so favourite a fighting ground that contractors could easily be found to undertake the business of furnishing transport and supply for an army; and sutlers were abundant. In Spain and Portugal no such contractors were forthcoming, and the Commissariat had to do the whole of the contractor's work for themselves. This was such a novelty that Wellington had to build up the whole system from the very foundation; and it was to his amazing talent for organisation quite as much as to his tactical and strategical ability that he owed his ultimate success.

At home the Treasury, which controlled the Commissariat, took three solid years to grasp that they were dealing with quite new conditions. They had been accustomed to provide the Army with a few clerks, who made and signed contracts and sent the accounts home, and they could not understand that, when the Commissariat did the work of the present Army Service Corps—as was the case in the Peninsula—it required a staff not of tens but of hundreds. The Commissariat provided the men with bread, meat and spirits; but even Wellington could not get on without sutlers. One was attached to every battalion or regiment, and he received from the Commissariat forage for two animals. It should be explained that, Portugal being practically roadless in those days, the transport consisted almost wholly of pack-mules. Two of these to each regimental sutler was not a large allowance, but it was as much as could possibly, in the circumstances, be granted.

THE SOLDIER'S CONDITION AFTER WATERLOO

In the course of the war a vast change had come over the life of the soldier at home. Barracks had been built on a very large scale in Great Britain, and the old system of billeting in ale-houses had come to an end. The British nation does not like changes; and, though the Army had won for the country a triumphant peace, it was very far from popular. The cost of the long war had been terrific. There was great distress at its close, alike in the manufacturing and agricultural industries, and consequently great and dangerous discontent. There was then no police, metropolitan or provincial; and the only power which stood between the country and anarchy was the Army. As police, officers and men alike showed astonishing forbearance, humanity and sympathy, but they were none the less loathed, because, for one thing, the cost of them was an item which contributed to crushing taxation, and for another they at least had full bellies while other men were starving.

In deference to the outcry of Parliament, vast numbers of soldiers were disbanded, and for a few years the establishment of the Army fluctuated violently between sudden augmentations and sudden reductions. Then it was recognised that the Army could not be lowered beneath a certain figure. A new empire had been won to replace that lost by the American rebellion. There were new acquisitions in India, Ceylon, Mauritius, the West Indies, the Mediterranean, the Cape, to say nothing of Australia, whose population was beginning to grow, and of New Zealand which was just coming over the horizon. And this new empire required protection, and not only protection but consolidation.

The bad times continued, with constant menaces of revolution in England and many outbreaks on the Continent, until 1849, and for long it was impossible to persuade Parliament to do anything for the Army. The formation of the Metropolitan Police in 1829 did something to relieve it of its

most unpleasant and unpopular work at home;
but abroad the needs of the Empire made constant
calls upon it, to which it was far too weak to
respond. The result was that it was shamefully
overworked. Battalions remained abroad for more
than twenty years unrelieved and, after four years
at home, were frequently sent abroad again. It
may be said that up to 1854 three out of four line
battalions, and sometimes even four out of five,
were always abroad, and not only abroad but
engaged in hard fighting in every kind of climate
with every description of hardship and privation.
None the less we now enter upon the period when,
through the exertions of officers, and chiefly of
regimental officers, steady progress was made in
improving the lot of the soldier.

THE BEGINNING OF BARRACK CANTEENS

Let us, however, first see how the State treated
him. The building of barracks brought up the
question of the sale of liquor in the barrack-yard.
It was so difficult to prevent men from smuggling
spirits into barracks that, as the less of two evils,
it was decided to allow spirits to be sold; and it
seems that private traders—probably old soldiers
or pensioners—were first permitted to set up a
canteen for the sale of spirits only. Then the
Board of Ordnance, being in charge of barracks,
took the matter in hand, and let the canteens to

contractors by tender for a term of three years. The system was that the contractor paid a fixed rent for the building, and a sum, known as "privilege money," which was a payment per month for every ten men in barracks at the beginning of the month. This "privilege money" was put up to competition; and contractors offered for it sums which they could not hope to make good by honest trade.

Other goods had by this time been added to the spirits; but of all alike the quality was bad and the prices high. The spirits in particular were rank fiery poison, more deadly and potent than were sold in ordinary public houses; and this was a fertile source of crime. Insubordination in barracks, and particularly the striking of non-commissioned officers, was very common, and was almost invariably the result of a visit to the canteen. On the other hand, the State through the letting of the canteens made no less than £53,000 a year, to the great satisfaction of Parliament, which did not reflect that against this profit was to be set the ruin of half a million's worth of good soldiers.

THE SOLDIER'S DIET

At home the soldier's ration was 1 lb. of bread and $\frac{3}{4}$ lb. of meat daily, for which 6d. a day was stopped from his pay. The cooking utensils to each company were two coppers, one for the potatoes and the other for the meat, which was always beef and always boiled, for there were no means of roasting or baking it. The soldier had two meals a day, breakfast at 7.30 and dinner at 12.30, so that he was left for nineteen hours without food. Since he lost appetite for the eternal beef-broth and boiled beef, he was naturally hungry and weak in the evening, and took refuge in drink. In the West Indies he had salt beef five days a week and fresh meat on two days. In Mauritius, where fresh meat was cheaper than salted, the fresh and the salted were given to him on alternate days. If by chance some salt pork in the naval stores required consumption, the soldier eagerly welcomed the change; but such a windfall was rare. He therefore consoled himself with drink.

In St Helena the men, if they worked at the construction of roads, received a quart of wine daily. In Mauritius they could get drunk for a penny. In the West Indies rum was 6d. a quart. At the Cape they could buy a bottle of wine for 2½d. and spirits at an equally reasonable rate. The Mediterranean garrisons produced similar temptations of cheap liquor. To be brief, the State offered every inducement in the way of monotonous diet, monotonous occupation, climatic discomfort, bad housing and abundant alcohol that could lure men to drink; and then deplored the drunkenness of the Army.

But meanwhile regimental officers worked busily to counteract the mischief of the State. In many regiments, regimental badges and medals were given to men of steady good character, thus encouraging the well-conducted by reward instead of only deterring the ill-conducted by punishment. The officers of the Guards, who were the only infantry that lived for any time at home, provided libraries for their literate men, gardens for the illiterate and savings-banks for all. Abroad the officers established savings-banks; but, having no funds, they could do little for their men except by their own exertions. And these assuredly they did not spare.

Thus it occurred to some of them that men drank from sheer exhaustion in the evenings, and they provided for them the means of obtaining cheap suppers and innocent coffee instead of wine. They did their best, moreover, though it was very difficult in those days, to furnish their soldiers with books. One colonel of Highlanders at the Cape formed a theatrical company from among his men, who took to the new recreation with enthusiasm and played their parts remarkably well. In fact the soldiers welcomed anything that offered any variation from the usual monotony; and the success which attended every effort of the officers showed that the men, or at any rate most of them, preferred to be sober and to lead quiet lives. But the officers were not rich, and the State carefully swept all the profits of the canteens into the public treasury.

THE STATE ADOPTS THE OFFICERS' IMPROVEMENTS

The evil dealing of the State and the counter-measures of the officers were all brought to light by a Commission[1]; and at last in 1836 the State began from very shame to learn from the officers. Good-conduct badges and good-conduct pay for the whole Army, instituted in 1836, was the first reform; and a larger allowance of fresh meat in the tropics was the second. In 1840 a third meal daily was made obligatory, the expense being stopped from the pay of the men, who, however, were allowed to make their own choice of trades-men and of one of themselves as caterer. In 1841 regimental savings-banks were established by re-gulation (the minister who announced this change was Macaulay the historian); and in 1847 it was openly proposed in the House of Commons that the existing regimental canteens should be replaced by coffee-rooms, and that the profit arising there-from should be devoted to the upkeep of reading-rooms and other institutions for the soldier's benefit.

The member who brought this forward was

[1] A Commission on Military Punishments.

Joseph Hume, a notorious character in his day, who by his incessant clamour for the reduction of the Army, had been the means—quite unconsciously—of killing thousands of soldiers through sheer prolongation of their stay in unhealthy climates. Moreover, his proposal that the profits of canteens should go to the men was not original. A very highly distinguished officer, Sir Henry Hardinge—one of the best friends that the British soldier ever had—had pointed out some years before that the canteens, as then conducted, were neither more nor less than a tax upon the private, and that this was not only an evil but a monstrous injustice. However, it was something to have gained Hume as an ally; and the effect was immediate.

BEGINNING OF CANTEEN REFORM

A few weeks later, several military members of the House opened their mouths to expose all the iniquities of the existing canteen-system and declared that improvement was impossible until not only the Government but the canteen-contractors ceased to make a profit out of the soldier's necessities. The answer from the Ministerial benches was feeble. Ministers did not defend the current practice. They could only say that it had grown up of itself. Canteens had been originally instituted to sell spirits only. They had gradually added to these other articles (presumably groceries) and, after all, commanding officers had full powers to deal with all evils. This characteristic endeavour to shelve the responsibility on the commanding officers was not, however, allowed to pass unchallenged. General de Lacy Evans, a veteran of the Peninsula who later commanded a division in the Crimea, testified that commanding officers had the strongest objection to the existing system, which was plain proof that their authority was insufficient to check its many mischiefs. In fact there was such fierce criticism that the Government announced that, on the expiration of the existing contracts, spirits should no longer be sold in canteens.

THE ESTABLISHMENT OF SOLDIERS' SCHOOLS

Meanwhile in this same year 1847 a beginning was made in another direction. The floating population of women and children attached to the Army all over the world numbered some ten thousand; and the proportion of illiterate men in the ranks was still about two in three. Normal and model regimental schools were established at Chelsea, where barracks had not long before been erected; and by 1851 regimental schools were flourishing and extending so fast that it was difficult to keep pace with the demand for teachers. Regimental libraries were also doing well. About one hundred thousand volumes had been acquired, and there were already sixteen thousand men subscribing to them. In fact it was clear that the soldier only wanted facilities for improving himself to grasp at them eagerly. It was the House of Commons which had been his real oppressor, by its combination of meanness with extortion. But the House of Commons was beginning to relent, though every concession required still to be fought for. Parliament would not at first grant the soldier even his good-conduct badges without fining him three shillings apiece for the price of every one that he earned. But gradually these and other grievances, many of them of long standing, were redressed, both for officers and men, and redressed with less and less sign of grudging, and more and more token of goodwill.

THE CRIMEAN WAR AND ITS LESSONS

Then in 1854 came the Crimean War, in which thousands of soldiers perished from sheer starvation and exposure. It was not the first campaign by any means in which such a thing had happened; but in 1854 there were war-correspondents on the spot, and the public for the first time realised the meaning of war. The main story is concerned rather with the history of the Army Service Corps than of canteens, and cannot be dealt with here. Exhaustive enquiry proved that the blame for all the administrative failures and disasters lay not with the military officers, but with the civil departments at home. But that is a detail. More important is the fact that the Crimean War for the first time brought the public into sympathetic touch with the Army. Folks at home were horrified by the sufferings of the soldiers, and deeply moved by the quiet patience with which they were endured.

VOLUNTARY EFFORT IN THE CRIMEA

Large subscriptions were raised, and generous men and women hurried to the base and to the hospitals to improve matters. Both, especially the women, who had been brought up to consider the soldier as a rough, drunken outcast, were astonished to find that he was gentle, courteous, unselfish and uncomplaining. Many establishments were opened to provide him with comforts, but for the most part they came too late, and, until they appeared, the Levantine trader alone was on the spot. His goods, as Lord Wolseley has, with much searching of heart, recorded, only officers could afford to buy. These same traders appear also to have set up their booths all the way along the eight miles between the base at Balaclava and the camp above Sebastopol. Of course, they sold liquor and, since the French shared all the work with the British—indeed after the first four months did far the larger portion of the work—the regulation of these traders was a matter of great difficulty, for the French in those days did not treat drunkenness as a crime, and the British did. It may therefore be said of the Crimean War, as of all previous wars, that for all comforts and luxuries the Army depended upon private adventurers.

ADMINISTRATIVE CHANGES

Vast changes, administrative and other, were effected in the Army during and immediately after the Crimean War, though the Indian Mutiny followed so closely upon it that the greater part of the Army was abroad, practically from 1854 till 1859. Foremost among these changes was the transfer of the Commissariat from the control of the Treasury to that of the War Office, and the establishment of what was called the Military Train, a forerunner of the present Army Service Corps. At the same time there was formed the camp at Aldershot, the ground having been purchased in 1853, and the camp itself opened in 1855. Until then there had never been troops enough gathered together in any one place, except at Dublin, to permit even of a brigade field-day. Much money was fooled away in building huts of green timber for the men, but, though the housing was not very grand, great improvements were made in the system of feeding the soldier. The Commissariat set up its own butcheries and bakeries, and, buying such groceries as tea, coffee, salt, pepper and the like in bulk, was able to furnish them to the men at Aldershot and to some stations abroad in return for a stoppage of 1½d. a day. But be it observed that it was only the concentration of troops in one spot which made such reforms possible.

Other simple remedies followed. Thus, instruction was given in cooking, though there were still in 1858 stations where soldiers were condemned to perpetual boiled beef, and could not get it baked or roasted unless by sending it out at their own expense. The sale of spirits in canteens, moreover, albeit nominally abolished, had by no means altogether ceased, though it was controlled by posting non-commissioned officers to stop drinking after the dinner hour. Some of the barracks, too, were still infamous, the buildings insanitary and the men shamefully overcrowded. But there was a group of members in the House of Commons which kept a sharp eye on these things, and they pressed continually not only for the abolition of evils, but for the amelioration of the soldier's lot by giving him recreation-rooms, fives-courts, cricket grounds and gymnasia. On the whole there was steady progress towards improvement.

Among other reforms, a change was made in the administration of the canteens. It was now decided that the tenant should pay rent for the building only and that the "privilege money"—or, in other words, the tax which was virtually levied upon the soldier for the privilege of buying within the barrack-yard—should be abandoned. It was represented that this improvement cost the country £26,000; though obviously it was not an additional charge on the nation but simply the renunciation of an iniquitous impost. However, the change proved to be no improvement. The old complaints of bad quality and high prices continued. The contractor or tenant profited largely at the cost of the soldier; and, as the result of experiments tried at Gibraltar and elsewhere, this system was in 1863 gradually displaced to make way for another that was to last nearly forty years.

NEW CANTEEN REGULATIONS OF 1863

The new regulations established the canteen as a regimental affair. The commanding officer selected a canteen-committee, consisting of a president, and two subordinates, and purchased his goods for the canteen in the open market from any tradesman or tradesmen selected by that committee. The steward, waiters, and barmen were generally drawn from the regiment; and the whole of the retail profits went to the regiment, being administered by the commanding officer, according to the best of his ability, for the benefit of his men. This was a long step in the right direction, and at first met with considerable success. Regimental officers took great pains to make it so; and in some cases they saved for each of their men a penny a day. The sum does not sound large, but in those days it was considered portentous.

Nevertheless, experience soon revealed grave disadvantages. The most serious of these were principally two. First, each unit, buying for itself, had to pay far more highly for goods which, by co-operation of many or of all units, might have been purchased more cheaply. Secondly, few officers had the knowledge and experience for handling what was really a strict matter of business, requiring skilled training. Some were careless; others were frightened; and in too many instances the canteens passed under the control of the canteen-stewards and non-commissioned officers. It was too much to expect of poor human nature that these last should not abuse their position to make illicit gain; and that some trading firms should not take advantage of the corruption thus introduced among canteens to increase their own profits.

Thus abuses sprang up quickly. A nervous canteen-president, conscious of his own ignorance, was glad to leave everything to an old canteen-steward who assured him that all had gone well since the canteen had dealt with Messrs A. & B.; while Messrs A. & B. assured him that he could not do better than maintain his old canteen-steward. If Messrs X. & Y. applied to the president for his custom, their only chance of obtaining it was to outbid Messrs A. & B. in bribes to the canteen-steward. Speaking generally, officers, distrusting their own competence, were content to allow existing arrangements to continue; and the canteen business, which had never enjoyed a very good name, by no means improved its reputation. Respectable firms, in fact, refused to have anything to do with it, and it was tending surely to become the monopoly of a few. The general result was serious loss to the British soldier.

SHORT SERVICE AND ITS INFLUENCE ON THE SOLDIER

After 1870[1] the Army slowly underwent complete transformation. Long service was abolished, and short service—first six years with the colours and six with the reserve, later seven or eight years with the colours and four or five with the reserve—was substituted for it. The change took some time to make itself felt, though our little wars between

1 In this same year the State made education free and compulsory, which practically opened to every private the possibility of gaining the stripes, and even a commission.

1870 and 1900 brought home to the public rather unpleasantly that the old soldier, who had made and consolidated the Empire, was gone for ever. Those thirty years of transition, when the old Army disappeared and the new was coming into being, were, from a military point of view, most dangerous, but were happily passed without serious mishap. In those days if anyone wanted to see a British battalion he had to go to India, where alone the ranks were full of matured men.

At home there were only raw boys, waiting until good food and physical training should raise them to the standard of their comrades in India. But these lads were very different from their long-service predecessors. The old soldiers had inherited traditions of hard drinking; and many of them returned to barracks night after night three parts drunk, though able to pass the guard without revealing their insobriety. They consumed a great deal of beer in the canteen; and, as everyone knows, no sale is so profitable as that of beer at the bar. The canteen-contractors, therefore, gave all possible encouragement to beer-drinking. But the young soldier was very different. He was born of a generation whose members, through nearly two centuries of natural selection, were ceasing to crave for alcohol. In all classes the same phenomenon was observed. In London clubs, and particularly in service clubs, it was noticed that

31

the younger men drank little or no wine; and, since clubs depended greatly on the sale of wine to make both ends meet, the fact caused some dismay among their financial committees. In the canteens the sale of beer steadily diminished; and here again the financial results of abstinence caused some embarrassment. But those who abstain from alcohol crave irresistibly for sugar; and sweet stuff in one form or another became essential to the health and nourishment of the soldier. Apart from this there had been steady advance in varying the soldier's diet—in itself a means (as has been seen) of averting the longing for stimulants. This variety had been effected principally through the canteens in time of peace; but no one could pretend that the general management of canteens was satisfactory.

MEASURES OF REGIMENTAL OFFICERS TO IMPROVE CANTEENS

Then once again the regimental officer interposed. There had always been some canteen-committees which did well for their own men, though these could not extend their benefactions beyond their own units. In 1892, however, the canteen-president of the 17th Lancers, Captain Lionel Fortescue, being dissatisfied with the situation as he took it over, instituted the practice of keeping a locked till in the canteen, sealing up change for the various silver coins, and insisting that every purchaser should place in the locked till the exact amount of his purchase. The contents of the till were counted every morning by an officer before the canteen opened; and it was found that the receipts were materially larger than they had been.

Then calculating the *minimum* of profit that should accrue to the canteen within a given number of weeks, Captain Fortescue ruthlessly dismissed every canteen-serjeant who showed a lower figure and, after getting rid of three in quick succession, found a man who worked heartily with him and took pride in earning as much as possible for the soldiers. The locked till was speedily copied by many regiments, and the discovery of the secrets of dishonest canteen-stewards proved valuable to all. The serjeant of the 17th Lancers, John Gardner, above referred to, had during the German War the handling of hundreds of thousands of pounds as one of the staff of the Navy and Army Canteen Board.

THE FOUNDING OF THE CANTEEN AND MESS CO-OPERATIVE SOCIETY

But this little administrative detail was a small matter to what was soon to come. In 1894 Major Harry James Craufurd, of the Grenadier Guards, then canteen-president of the Guards' Depot at Caterham, being dissatisfied with the source from which the canteen was supplied, consulted two of his friends, Captain Lionel Fortescue aforesaid, and Surgeon-Captain Herbert Murray Ramsay, medical officer attached to the Scots Guards. They agreed that the best way to obtain supplies at a reasonable figure was to form a co-operative society, registered under the Industrial and Provident Societies Act and affiliated to the Co-operative Union. They and a few of their friends, all poor men, then collected £400 and founded the Canteen and Mess Co-operative Society. Under its rules no individual was allowed to hold more than £200 worth of shares; the interest thereon was limited to 5 per cent., and all profits in excess of that interest were to be returned, by way of rebate, to the regimental canteens that were its customers. Mr Charles Heygate, a friend of Major Craufurd, was consulted by him as to starting the business, and in 1895 took over the duties of secretary himself.

The new Society at first occupied small premises in the east end of London; and its first year's turnover did not exceed £4700. But the advantages which it offered were quickly discovered by regiments, and, despite fierce competition from the firms which had enjoyed the monopoly of canteen business, its trade steadily increased. In 1896 the Society moved to much larger premises in Regency Street, Westminster; and very soon Captain Fortescue, enlarging upon Major Craufurd's original idea, conceived of a plan by which he hoped to place the Society upon a much stronger footing. This was that the customer-regiments should gradually buy out the individual shareholders, making the Society their own; that eventually the whole Army should be included, and that the Society should be the whole Army's Co-operative Society, conducting its own business for its own officers and men, and distributing the profits, both wholesale and retail, among them without any official interference whatever. The scheme was derided by most officers as an idle dream, but Captain Fortescue never lost faith in it.

THE SOUTH AFRICAN WAR 1899–1902. NEW CANTEEN REGULATIONS

In the autumn of 1899 the South African War broke out and, owing to the removal of the greater part of the Army to South Africa, new regulations were promulgated for canteens. Two alternative systems were allowed:

(1) The REGIMENTAL TENANT SYSTEM, under which the supply both of the liquor and the grocery bars was given out by the commanding officer to tender; the tender of the firm which offered the highest rebate to the customer-regiment being as a rule accepted. The contracting

firm bound itself to furnish not only the supplies but the working staff for the canteen.

(2) The DISTRICT CONTRACT SYSTEM, which removed the selection of the supplying firm from the regimental commanding officers to the district commanding officer, who contracted on behalf of all the units within his command. Thereby was gained the advantage of purchasing on a large scale; but, on the other hand, the working staff was provided by the various units, and thus an appreciable number of soldiers were diverted from their legitimate duties.

The Canteen and Mess Society secured three district contracts, and in 1900 the volume of its trade rose to £265,000.

THE CANTEEN AND MESS SOCIETY IN SOUTH AFRICA

At the same time the Society did not neglect the seat of war. The South African campaign was just such another as that of the American rebellion, being carried on over an enormous territory against an elusive enemy, in which much hardship and fatigue were inevitable, success not very exhilarating and reverses extremely galling. It was conducted from two principal bases a thousand miles apart, Capetown and Durban. Capetown lay a thousand and Durban five hundred miles from the extreme limits of the enemy's country; and the operations, if undertaken under the same conditions as in 1775, without steamships and railways, must inevitably have failed. The work was so thankless and so empty of reward that the troops needed every possible little luxury or comfort to hearten them to go through it; and, if the war had taken place a century earlier, any enterprising sutlers would have made a fortune.

The Government had not thought of the part formerly played by sutlers. The new canteen-regulations offered no solution of the problem. It was impossible for forty or fifty regimental contractors to take the field with the troops, and it was equally impossible to spare soldiers from the fighting line to tend canteen-bars. But the regiments which were clients of the Canteen and Mess Co-operative Society, more far-seeing than the Government, asked the Society to place a certain number of canteen-stores upon every troopship that conveyed their units to the seat of war, and further to supplement these supplies by regular shipments to South Africa. The Society complied, and sent out further a small staff to be responsible for the distribution of the goods.

In due time it came to the ears of Lord Roberts, who commanded on the Capetown side, that some of his regiments were receiving luxuries which were not enjoyed by others. He made enquiry, and found that the fortunate units were those who were members of the Canteen and Mess Society. Thereupon he cabled to ask if the Society would supply the whole of the troops as well as its own members. The Society assented, provided that certain facilities were granted to it. The terms were agreed upon, and the Society opened a new depot, increased its staff and continued to do its work until the two armies of Lord Roberts, on the Capetown side, and of Sir Redvers Buller, on the Durban side, joined hands, as from the converging direction of their advance they were bound sooner or later to do. Then it was found that Sir Redvers Buller had formed a military organisation of his own called "The Natal Field Force Canteen." The question thereupon arose whether of the two, the Canteen and Mess Society or the Natal Field Force Canteen, should be continued. It was decided that the military organisation should prevail. The Natal Field Force Canteen, rechristened by the new name of the South African Garrison Institutes, took over the stock and staff of the Canteen and Mess Society, and the Society was relegated to such work as might be left to it among the few troops at home.

HUGH, FOURTH EARL FORTESCUE

Thus, suddenly cut off from its activities in South Africa, for the furtherance of which it had incurred heavy financial responsibility, the Society found itself in serious straits. Of its leading spirits Major Fortescue had been killed in action in June 1900; Major Craufurd was in failing health; and Captain Ramsay was very fully occupied with his profession. Moreover, all three were poor men, and what was needed was capital. The few firms which held most of the canteen business foresaw with satisfaction the downfall of their most serious rival, the Society which worked not for its own profit but for the soldier's. It seemed as if the Canteen and Mess Society must succumb.

Happily a friend was found in Mr J. F. Herring, the well-known philanthropist and financier. He looked into the records of the Society, and being well pleased with the work that it had done and was doing, he decided to support it. He therefore went to the Society's bankers, and told them that, if they would be content to wait for better times, he would himself be answerable for any money that might be required from that date onward. At the same time Lord Fortescue, who had from the first shown a lively interest in the Society for his brother's sake, now undertook a more active part in the management. He was in fact the first chairman of the committee of the Society, and he now took his brother's place and retained his connection with the co-operative movement until 1919.

With Mr Herring's timely and invaluable help and encouragement the Canteen and Mess Society gathered new life. While the Army remained in South Africa, difficulties continued; but they were gradually overcome. It may be said here briefly that Mr Herring was never called upon to make good his guarantee, and that within little more than two years the Society had repaid the whole of its liabilities to its bankers and was once more upon firm ground.

The termination of the South African War in 1902 of course contributed materially to this result. But that war had been attended by many rather humiliating little reverses, and there was much clamour among the public that the reasons for these mishaps should be enquired into and discovered. There had been similar agitation during and after the Crimean War, not without good results; though, as a matter of fact, the reason for the initial failure in both cases could have been explained by any sensible man in a single sentence. It was simply that the country had undertaken a military enterprise beyond the strength of the military force which, in defiance of all military opinion, it had maintained as sufficient for its needs.

However, nothing would satisfy the public but a number of costly Commissions of Enquiry; and, among others, a committee was set up to consider the existing conditions under which canteens, or to give them their longer title, Regimental Institutes, were conducted.

LORD GREY'S CANTEEN COMMITTEE

This committee, known from the name of its chairman as Lord Grey's Committee, after questioning a great number of witnesses, issued their report in 1903, to the following effect:

That commanding officers of regiments should be permitted to choose between managing their canteens on the old regimental system, as before the South African War, or handing them over to a Soldiers' Central Co-operative Society to be formed on the model [though this was not expressly so stated] of the Canteen and Mess Co-operative Society. The Commander-in-Chief, or his nominee, was to be the Chairman of the General Committee of Management of this Soldiers' Central Co-operative Society, and the books were to be audited by chartered accountants appointed by the War Office.

The report, however, was not unanimous. Two out of the eight members of the committee dissented from the recommendation respecting the Soldiers' Central Co-operative Society, and stated their reasons in a minority report. One of them,

Lord Cheylesmore, an old officer of the Grenadier Guards, had laboured hard all his life for the soldier and had done admirable work; but he could not bring himself to believe in such a novelty, and he said so with uncompromising honesty. Nor were such opinions confined to him. Many officers—perhaps practically all above a certain age—however zealous for the soldiers' welfare, were mistrustful of any such experiment as a Central Soldiers' Co-operative Society. They knew little or nothing of the co-operative movement, and especially scouted the suggestion that any commanding officer should invest the profits of his canteen in any co-operative society.

THE TENANCY SYSTEM CONTINUED

So matters were left as they were, and the "Tenant System," under which canteens were let out to contractors, was continued. The outward attraction of this system was the rebate which the contractor undertook to pay; but its inward defect was that contractors could pick and choose the canteens which it would be remunerative to conduct, and in many cases could dictate the rate of rebate which they would grant. The less profitable canteens—those of small units in outlying stations—had difficulty in finding contractors to take their business at all. In fact, with the restoration of a system already discredited, all the old abuses returned.

Apart from the Canteen and Mess Society and at least one notable contracting firm, bribery and corruption flourished. The quality of goods delivered was poor, and the soldier suffered. The only safeguard essayed by the authorities was to limit the choice of contractors by commanding officers to a definite list of firms; and this, as shall presently be seen, proved to be painfully illusory.

THE CANTEEN AND MESS SOCIETY'S MODIFICATION THEREOF

The Canteen and Mess Co-operative Society was included in the list, but, having no belief in the tenancy system, it evolved, always under the guidance of Mr Heygate, a modification of its own. Under this system the Society charged any canteen for its supplies at the rate of its wholesale price-lists, and submitted its retail price-lists for the commanding officer's approval. The Society furnished the working staff and paid the working expenses; and, after deduction of these from the retail profits, it handed the balance over to the commanding officer together with the monthly balance sheet. In this way the regiment concerned was sure of getting the whole of its profits, and not a mere arbitrary rebate. If for any reason the commanding officer desired to make a little more money for his men, he could do so by raising the retail prices; but the Society, working on co-operative principles, had no object in raising retail prices for itself, since all profits, whether greater or less, after deduction of working expenses, returned automatically to the regiment.

THE CANTEEN SCANDAL OF 1914

Offering these advantages, only possible, it must be noted, in a co-operative society, the Canteen and Mess forged slowly ahead, until in 1914 an accidental occurrence brought it prominently forward. In 1913–14 the eyes of the military authorities were opened by what was known as "the Canteen Scandal." It is unnecessary to rake up the details of a half-forgotten and wholly discreditable story. Suffice it that there were allegations of bribes offered by individual employees of a firm approved by the War Office, and of the acceptance of those bribes by some of its military customers; and that the matter culminated in a prosecution. Therein those allegations were conclusively established, and, as a consequence, certain officers and non-commissioned officers were dismissed from the Army.

The press took the scandal up warmly and, forgetting the enquiry instituted by Lord Grey's Committee only eleven years before, urged strongly an investigation of the whole subject of canteens by Government. A strong committee, which counted among its members Lord Rotherham for

44

chairman, Lord Leverhulme and Sir R. Burbidge, was appointed to deal finally with the whole matter. Meanwhile the exposure of malpractice on the part of one of the War Office's approved firms gave a powerful impulse to the co-operative movement. Regimental Institutes turned eagerly to the Canteen and Mess Society, whose business made rapid advances.

THE GERMAN WAR 1914–1918

In August 1914 all arrangements were upset by the outbreak of the German War. The Expeditionary Force—or in other words, the greater part of the Regular Army—was sent to France, and the youth of England turned out by hundreds of thousands to make a new army. Demands upon canteens were doubled and trebled; and the Canteen and Mess Society was flooded with work. As in South Africa in 1899, so in France in 1914, no provision had been made by the military authorities for any canteen-organisation in the field. In France and Flanders local tradesmen saw their opportunity and raised their prices; and the General in command begged urgently for some arrangement to make good the crying needs of his troops. It had been forgotten that in all previous European wars sutlers had come forward to supplement the work of the Commissariat, and that quite recently in South Africa the Army had made its own field-force canteens. Not all of our administrators are blessed with good memories.

FOUNDATION OF THE EXPEDITIONARY FORCE CANTEEN

In this emergency the War Office summoned the head of the Canteen and Mess Society and the managing director of the soundest and most experienced firm of canteen-contractors, and threw itself upon their mercy. The Canteen and Mess Society thereupon formed a special department to deal with this business, adding a special provision that Sir Alexander Prince, chairman and managing director of Richard Dickeson & Co.—the contracting firm in question—should be asked to act as honorary director of that department. Sir Alexander consented, to the great gain of everyone concerned; and thus the association of the contractors and of the Canteen and Mess Society, formerly rivals, was happily effected.

THE CANTEEN AND MESS SOCIETY TAKES THE LEAD

Nevertheless the Society naturally took the lead. It was the only co-operative canteen-organisation whose constitution bound it to work, not for shareholders, but wholeheartedly for its members—the soldiers—and therefore it stood alone. The whole of the staff was appointed and the whole of the

business was conducted by the Canteen and Mess
Society; and so came into being the Expeditionary
Force Canteen, more famous under its familiar
initials E.F.C.

Its first need was money, for the Canteen and
Mess Society, founded as it had been by poor
men, had never had more than £12,000 of capital.
A first instalment of £10,000, subsequently increased to £27,000, was taken from the funds of
the South African Garrison Institutes. Those Institutes, it will be remembered, were evolved from
the Natal Field Force Canteen; and their funds
were not the State's money, nor contractors'
money, but the soldiers' money; exactly as were
the funds of the Canteen and Mess Society. Such
a trifling sum was of course wholly inadequate,
and was presently supplemented by bank over-
drafts and by loans, guaranteed by the Treasury,
to the total amount of £720,000. It may be said
here once for all that these loans were all repaid
with due interest.

THE BOARD OF CONTROL OF REGIMENTAL INSTITUTES

We shall presently follow the career of the E.F.C.
more closely; but first we must glance at the course
of events at home. With the armies abroad upon
their hands the Canteen and Mess Society and
Messrs R. Dickeson & Co. could not at once

extend their business to meet all the needs of the troops training in the United Kingdom. Recruits were pouring in daily by thousands; they needed canteens; and a host of contractors sprang up like mushrooms for the express purpose of trading with them and enriching themselves at the soldier's expense. It was recognised that some safeguard was needed to protect the soldier's interests, and Lord Rotherham's Committee suggested the appointment of a Board to supervise the operations of all these contractors. Accordingly, in January 1915, about five months after the declaration of war, a body was set up under the title of the Board of Control of Regimental Institutes.

The Board was formed to carry out the following duties:

(1) To allow no one to supply the troops except approved firms of contractors.

(2) To fix the retail prices which were to govern the supplies of all contractors.

(3) To secure a flat rate of rebate of 10 per cent. from every contractor, or, if the contractor had put up his own premises, then $7\frac{1}{2}$ per cent. on the takings.

It must be remembered that the system which had brought up the "canteen scandal" still remained unaltered, though it stood condemned; and the efforts thus to prolong its life were not very successful. Side by side with the Board there was formed, within a branch of the Quarter-Master General's department, a body of officers who acted as canteen-inspectors. These were responsible for supervising the conduct of canteens and for maintaining the good quality of the goods supplied by them. But it was soon found impossible for the Board and these inspectors to work independently of each other; and they were consequently amalgamated under the name of the Army Canteen Committee. This, however, mended matters but little. As the war was prolonged, the difficulty of obtaining certain kinds of supplies became greater; and it was found that the mere supervision of upstart contractors by no means sufficed to protect the soldier from bad goods and high prices.

THE ARMY CANTEEN COMMITTEE

Something must be done; and once again the Canteen and Mess Society showed the way. The huge success of the Expeditionary Force Canteen (presently to be related) suggested the application of the Society's principles to all canteens at home. Accordingly, in October 1916, the Army Canteen Committee recommended that the old system of tenancy in canteens should be abolished and that all canteens should be conducted by a central organisation which should be owned and controlled by the Army itself. On the 1st of January

1917, accordingly, the Army Canteen Committee was registered at the Board of Trade as "a company, not for profit" and limited by guarantee, but otherwise embracing every principle which the Canteen and Mess Society had practised and advocated for years.

This done, the Army Canteen Committee began to take over all business from the civil contractors, and to establish itself as a central organisation not only for general control but for the provision of supplies. In the process it may be said to have absorbed all the organised contracting firms, including Messrs R. Dickeson & Co., the strongest and most important of all. The Canteen and Mess Society likewise disappeared in name, but merely in name; for the Army Canteen Committee absorbed not only its organisation (excepting the Expeditionary Force Canteen), but its spirit, its traditions and its practice. Sir Alexander Prince gracefully sacrificed, on behalf of Messrs R. Dickeson & Co., the permanent interests of his business for the common good; and the union of that firm with the Canteen and Mess Society made the nucleus out of which the gigantic organisation of the Army Canteen Committee was expanded.

THE NAVY AND ARMY CANTEEN BOARD

By April 1917 over two thousand canteens were being conducted by the Army Canteen Committee. At about the same time it spread its arms far over sea, and took over all canteens in Gibraltar, Malta and Egypt proper.

In June 1917 the Navy asked that the British sailor might share in the benefits thus conferred on the British soldier, and was readily welcomed. Thereupon the Committee assumed the new title of the Navy and Army Canteen Board. In April 1918, when the Royal Air Force was constituted into a separate service, its canteens also passed by agreement of the Air Ministry under the control of the Navy and Army Canteen Board. Captain Fortescue, in the early days of the Canteen and Mess Society, had dreamed of a co-operative canteen-system which should make the canteens the property of the officers and men of the Army. And now within eighteen years of his death not the Army only, but every officer and man of the fighting services had been gathered into the fold.

Capital was of course needed to finance so colossal an undertaking; and the Treasury guaranteed at the outset a bank overdraft of two millions, which was increased to three millions as business grew. And business did not fail to grow. The Board, to avoid useless competition, purchased many goods for the Expeditionary Force Canteens for one item, and this was not a small one; but, apart from that, the Board's turnover at home alone in the year 1918 exceeded 40 millions. One has only to question those whose duties or disabilities condemned them to wear khaki in the British Isles only, during the war, to find out what an inestimable boon to all ranks were the canteens at the great camps in England.

THE EXPEDITIONARY FORCE CANTEEN

THE WESTERN FRONT

But let us now return from the great Central Board of 1917 to what may be called its true predecessor, the Expeditionary Force Canteen, which in 1915 was created and conducted entirely by the Canteen and Mess Society. It is curious to read of its small beginnings at Havre in February 1915. Its transport consisted of a single secondhand Ford car; and there was no hint of the fleet of automobiles into which this primitive vehicle was eventually to expand. Nevertheless, in the spring of 1915 there were already half a million troops on the Western Front, and, as their needs became clearer, so did the activity of the E.F.C. increase. In the first six months of 1915 the sales of the E.F.C.'s depots and canteens amounted to only three millions of francs; by the end of the year they had swelled to 18 millions; in the first six months of 1916 they reached 48 millions; in the last six months they exceeded 104 millions. Between January and July 1917 they rose to 150 millions;

from July to December 1917 they reached 191 millions, and in the last year of the war, 1918, they attained their climax of 223 millions of francs. And these, it must be noted, were good tenpenny francs, five and twenty to the pound sterling, not the depreciated twopenny franc of 1928, one hundred and twenty-four to the pound sterling.

In the course of those four years the E.F.C. became literally universal providers for all the wants of the Army and of its auxiliary services at the Western Front. More and more base-depots were established, until they attained to their final total of seventeen for as many areas; and each of these pushed out its tentacles to the front almost into the firing line, till, at the moment of its greatest expansion, the E.F.C. had no fewer than 577 branches in France and Flanders. The goods supplied ranged from a button to a bottle of champagne, and from a packet of pins to complete equipment for an officer. To give but a single example of the task of distribution it may be mentioned that the solitary Ford car at Havre had by 1918 been replaced by 249 lorries and vans, 151 cars, 42 motor cycles and 14 trailers. It is an old proverb in the lore of transport and supply that any fool can fill a depot; but that it needs a man to bring food to the soldier's mouth. There were many such men in the E.F.C.

CASUALTIES OF THE E.F.C.

Nor were they exempt from the perils of war. Let us glance at them first at the extreme front. During the German advance in the spring of 1918 between sixty and seventy canteens were wiped out; but their work was carried on to the very last moment. In many cases troops were served under heavy shell-fire, and the canteen was never abandoned until for military reasons evacuation became imperative, and its premises were needed for a field-dressing station. Even then there was no disorder nor indiscipline. The men of the E.F.C. worked steadily to remove as many of the stores as possible and to destroy those that could not be carried away. In one case fifty shells fell within as many yards of premises from which they were clearing goods; in another they loaded trucks while gas-shells were actually falling on the rail-head. When they could do no more, some drifted back, starving, to the base to reopen fresh canteens which should replace those destroyed; others volunteered to act as stretcher-bearers; others again received rifles and joined the fighting troops. Many were killed or wounded, and not a few earned medals for meritorious service; yet the quantity of their stores that fell into German hands was, relatively speaking, extremely small.

REST-HOUSES AND LEAVE-BILLETS

But it was behind the lines that the chief work of the E.F.C. was done. Rest-houses and officers' clubs were required in 1917 for the recuperation of those who returned exhausted from the trenches, and to these were added "leave-billets" or in other words provision for the comfort at the base-ports of all men going on or returning from furlough, and of all reinforcements both British and, later, American. The military authorities threw themselves upon the E.F.C. to supply what was needed; and the E.F.C. made no difficulty over responding. It spread the table—as has been happily said—for the entire British Expeditionary Force, from the mess at General Headquarters to the private soldiers' billets. Everything that could be thought of to make men forget the horrors of the front was to be found at these clubs and rest-houses; not merely good fare—though there is no more comforting change to a war-worn man than change of diet—but neatness, cleanliness, comeliness and attention, in fact all that could most agreeably contrast with emergency-rations and the sound and smell of slaughter.

It is true that even by the sea the enemy pursued the E.F.C. with bombing aeroplanes and the like mischief. More than one rest-house was blown to pieces; but in such cases another was at once provided in substitution for it, and the work went

55

on as before. Whatever might happen, the E.F.C. meant to "carry on"; and not the least remarkable part of its history is its resourcefulness.

FACTORIES

At the outset, as its name implies, the E.F.C. undertook only to provide the troops with such little comforts or luxuries as were associated with the name of "canteen" at home. It may not seem very remarkable, therefore, that it should have set up its own mineral-water-factory very early in the day, and have taken over in 1915 the Valroy Springs at Étaples for the general supply of the Army. Wherever British troops were, there was Valroy water obtainable at a trifling cost, which, added to lime-juice cordial or some like preparation (also produced at Étaples factory), became the regular summer drink of the Army.

Those who, like the present writer, have some knowledge of the past campaigns of the British Army, can appreciate the vast amount of internal disease that must have been averted by the omnipresence of a pure and wholesome drink. Not that the soldier was condemned to non-alcoholic beverages only, for the E.F.C. also brewed its own beer for the men, and gathered in wine for the officers direct from growers not only in France but also in Italy, Spain and Portugal. But pure drinking-water everywhere means a great deal to an army.

WORKS AND OTHER DEPARTMENTS

Since butcheries and bakeries are normal appurtenances of an army in the field, they must be passed over lightly, though the bakeries produced far more tempting fare than would have been dreamed of in the Peninsula or in the Crimea. But, owing to the vast areas and the huge numbers of men to be supplied, the E.F.C. was confronted with a constant succession of fresh problems, which were solved as soon as they presented themselves. Thus suitable buildings were not always to be found at convenient places for depots and such like. The E.F.C. promptly started a Works Department and erected the edifice that was required. Its exterior might not always be very imposing, but the interior was always comfortable. The fitting up of the interior called into existence an Upholstery Department; while an Equipment Department was charged with the duty of providing the tons of crockery and kindred matters that were needed for canteens, rest-houses and the like.

THE PRINTING DEPARTMENT

Then again the requirements of so gigantic an organisation as the E.F.C. necessitated a vast amount of printing. The E.F.C. without hesitation installed its own printing machines in France, and found plenty of occupation for them. One of its greatest feats was accomplished at the end of the war, when General Headquarters suddenly announced the unexpected arrival of tens of thousands of our released prisoners, half starved and without a penny in their pockets. An order for half a million vouchers, entitling officers and men to free goods from any E.F.C. canteen, was placed with the Printing Department, and in a few hours these vouchers were handed over the counter by the prisoners, who received articles to the value printed upon them. Had not the printers and the printing press been on the spot, this sudden inrush of released prisoners must have led to great confusion.

THE CINEMA DEPARTMENT

Yet another strange extraneous branch of the E.F.C. was the Cinema Department. An essential element in the refreshment of the soldier, when withdrawn from the fighting line, was mental distraction, supplementary to the physical changes of diet, comfort and environment. The various units of the Army, well aware of this, first obtained films from firms in London and Paris, and were not at the outset very willing to transfer their custom to the E.F.C. A few weeks' experience, however, sufficed to convince them that the E.F.C. furnished an infinitely better service than could be obtained elsewhere; and, up to the beginning of the German offensive in March 1918, the E.F.C.'s Cinema Department was supplying to various units two hundred and forty films per week.

But the department soon passed beyond its original purpose of merely furnishing films. It was obvious that cinematographic machinery and generating sets for the provision of electric light (for the projection of films) were also required; and these were speedily produced. Over one hundred and seventy units purchased generating plant and cinema outfits and received in return engineers and operators free of charge. Wherever it was possible, cinema theatres were opened and conducted by the E.F.C., but these were unfortunately few owing to their lack of the necessary hands.

After the great German offensive of 1918 most of the theatres were perforce closed; whereupon the E.F.C., not to be beaten, organised six mobile cinemas, and gave entertainment to the troops, free of charge, as near to the fighting line as was possible. When the war came to an end, the E.F.C. opened cinema-houses at all places, such as demobilisation-camps and ports of embarkation, where many troops were gathered together, continuing this service to the very end.

In chronological order the expedition to the Dardanelles should next claim our attention, but it will be better to have done with the activities of the E.F.C. in Western Europe. From France the natural transition is to Italy, which was used first as a country of passage to the East and later as an actual theatre of operation for a comparatively small body of British troops. The route to the East was marked by the following stages—Southampton to Cherbourg, Cherbourg to St Germain Mont d'Or (a little to the north of Lyon), St Germain to Faenza, Faenza to Taranto. There were rest-camps at St Germain, Faenza and Taranto, at which last place there was an ice-factory and a mineral-water-factory; and the E.F.C. supplied food and other necessaries for all the hundreds of thousands of troops passing over the thousand miles of train journey from Cherbourg.

For the troops actually engaged in Italy, the base was at Arquata, about forty miles north of Genoa. The E.F.C. arrived there and opened its doors for business only four days after the troops, eventually establishing there six canteens. It furnished also canteens on the lines of communication, radiating from Arquata to Cremona on the east, Milan in the north, Turin to the west and Ventimiglia to the south-west, with rest-houses and larger depots at various points, where cinemas (much patronised by the Italian troops) were set up as well as supply-stores. For the remoter posts there were five large travelling canteens—shops on wheels—which visited outlying units every week. Lastly, when the troops pushed on to the Piave and thence to the Asiago plateau, the E.F.C. went with them carrying their comforts.

Such is the bald story in a very few lines, giving little idea of the energy and forethought in overcoming a thousand difficulties in order that the British soldier might be well supplied, and so kept cheerful and happy. If the E.F.C. had done no work save this in Italy alone, it could boast of a very great achievement; but probably few civilians are aware that it did any work there at all.

THE E.F.C. AT GALLIPOLI

If ever troops needed compensation for incessant hardship and danger, it was those that were engaged in the ill-starred expedition to Gallipoli. Excellent in strategic conception, the enterprise was wrecked by imperfect preparation at home. The E.F.C. appeared on the spot in August 1915, nearly four months after the original disembarkation, and set up a canteen at Helles under perpetual shell-fire. No sooner did this attain to respectable proportions than it was blown to pieces; and the E.F.C. perforce limited itself to canteens at Suvla and on the islands of Imbros and Lemnos. Happily abundant supplies came in at the period

of the evacuation, whereby many lives were doubt-
less saved. For there was much sickness abroad,
the men were dispirited by failure, and a few
luxuries did much to hearten them.

THE E.F.C. AT SALONIKA

After the evacuation of Gallipoli many of the
troops were transferred to Salonika, and the E.F.C.
of course went with them to set up, not only
the usual canteens, with ice- and mineral-water-
factories, but rest-houses, officers' clubs and the
inevitable cinema-shows. At one time it had
thirty-five canteens along the line of the sixty
miles from the river Vardar eastward to the Gulf
of Orfano; and, in the sweltering heat of the
summer, ice and aerated water (of which it
turned out over ten thousand bottles a day) were
a priceless comfort to the healthy, and still more
to the sick. With a fleet of some forty automobiles
of one kind and another, and with ox-transport
where the roads would not permit automobiles to
travel, it contrived somehow to bring the food
and drink to the mouth. When the advance came,
the canteens were never far behind the troops, and
managed to keep in touch with them even to Sofia.
For the rest, due care was taken that the Indian
soldiers should fare as well as their British comrades; the E.F.C. importing the foods, which were
specially to their taste, from its depot at Bombay.

In Egypt again the E.F.C. followed the troops; at first as itself, and later in the form of the Navy and Army Canteen Board. Various causes conspired to make the collection of supplies a matter of extreme difficulty; but after a time all obstacles were overcome, and a line of canteens sprang up along the banks of the Suez Canal. Thence the E.F.C. pushed its way slowly but steadily across the desert, until at last in Palestine there appeared, within a mile of the fighting line, a chain of kiosks where the men could buy for three halfpence a pint of tea, or of coffee, or of aerated drinks, or two packets of cigarettes, with other articles at equally low rates.

THE E.F.C. IN MESOPOTAMIA

Of all the spheres of British operations, Mesopotamia was perhaps the most forbidding, and that was where the services of the E.F.C. were most urgently required. Ice and mineral waters there are not luxuries but necessities. The base here was at Basra, and, since the principal means of communication was by water, the E.F.C. soon set up a floating canteen on a stern-wheel steamboat. There were at one time thirty-seven canteens in Mesopotamia, going up the Euphrates and Tigris from Basra to Bagdad, beyond which they spread out fanwise to north and south and even into Persia. The greatest feat of the E.F.C. was after the capture of Kut-el-Amara by Sir Stanley Maude, when it had a floating canteen tied up to the bank at Azizeyeh, within an hour of the evacuation of that village by the Turks. One can imagine how welcome must have been its appearance to the weary and thirsty troops. In Mesopotamia, as in other eastern spheres, the same care was taken to provide for Indian as for native troops; and there, as elsewhere, the cinema supplied distraction for both.

Here once again is but a bare bald record, which takes no account of intense heat, swarms of flies, many different nationalities of oriental employees and the thousand impediments which make life a burden and labour an inferno.

THE N.A.C.B. WITHIN THE ARCTIC CIRCLE

The aftermath of the war finally led the Navy and Army Canteen Board to the Murmansk Coast of Northern Russia, within the Arctic Circle, where its operations were chiefly confined to the base; and to Archangel, where it followed the troops right up to the lines, five hundred miles from the base.

THE UBIQUITY OF THE CANTEENS

In fact, wherever the King's soldiers went, there the canteens followed them, whether to the Arctic Circle or to the Equator. The question is often asked, "Who won the war?" and it must be admitted that the E.F.C. did its share towards the great work by helping to keep the British soldier in good moral as well as in good physical condition. The present writer who is familiar with the past campaigns of the British Army—the campaigns which won the British Empire—has too often had before him the picture of British soldiers dying like flies from yellow fever, cholera, scurvy, enteric fever, dysentery (the two last frequently the result of bad food), heat, cold, starvation and, sometimes, sheer despair. He can, therefore, form some idea of the tens of thousands of lives that must have been saved by the labours of the E.F.C., to say nothing of the confidence that must have been inspired by its ubiquity.

THE HIGHER RANKS OF THE E.F.C.

One is left wondering how any human organisation can have overcome so gigantic a task as that of following our millions of British soldiers through their many wanderings between 1914 and 1918, and, amid all the complexities and surprises of military operations, bringing their comforts and luxuries to their feet. Millions of tons of supplies of all kinds had to be collected from England, from America, Australia, India and Japan, and distributed all over the world; and this at a time when the sea was unsafe and ships were sent to the bottom by scores and hundreds. The task of the central administration was enough to make any brain reel, but it was accomplished; and from the very highest to the lowest all strove equally to achieve the great object of keeping the British soldier healthy and cheerful in the field. And they strove with success.

The fact is that the E.F.C. had in its ranks some of the very best business-brains in England, men who, whether fit and liable for military service or not, had learned in their ordinary vocations in England to manage large concerns of one kind or another and, for such difficult work as the higher administrative problems of the E.F.C., were simply invaluable. Hotel-managers and restaurant-managers made light of conducting a rest-house of two hundred beds and four thousand daily meals, and of furnishing in the leave-camps over ten million meals in ten months to reinforcements and furlough-men, both British and American. But because these things were well done, it does not follow that they were easy to do.

THE LOWER RANKS OF THE E.F.C.

In the lower grades of the organisation, one most remarkable point is the very small staffs which contrived at some of the busiest stations to accomplish, and continue to accomplish, wonderful work. But more remarkable still is the list of businesses and trades from which, first and last, the staff was drawn. There were accountants, bakers, billiard-cushion repairers, billiard markers, brewers, butchers, builders, carpenters, chefs, chiropodists, cinema-operators check-takers and managers, clerks, compositors, confectioners, cooks, drapers, draughtsmen, dressmakers, engineers (electrical, hot water and gas), engravers, firemen, fishmongers, fruiterers, glaziers, grocers, hairdressers, hotel- and restaurant-managers, interpreters, joiners, kitchen-clerks, maîtres d'hôtel, mineral-water engineers bottlers and corkers, motor-transport drivers (steam and petrol) and repairers, piano-tuners, reception-clerks, sausage pork-pie and brawn makers, sports games and athletic equipment assistants, stenographers, syrup-makers, tailors, telephone-operators, tent-makers and repairers, upholsterers, waiters, wine experts, and works clerks—a tale of some fifty callings of infinite variety.

GOOD WORK OF THE W.A.A.C.

It must be added that the E.F.C. received valuable assistance from the Women's Auxiliary Army Corps, which provided great numbers of clerks, motor-drivers, cooks, waitresses, saleswomen and maids. They, as the rest of the staff, took the risk of bombing raids, of which they underwent several, sometimes seeing the whole of their possessions destroyed and on one occasion eight of their number killed by a single shell. But they never failed in their duty, raid or no raid. Special canteens were opened for them by the E.F.C. for the supply, among other things, of uniform clothing; and thus it is that the item dressmakers has been added to the foregoing list of trades.

THE E.F.C. SELF SUPPORTING

And now comes the most remarkable detail of all. The work of the E.F.C., the value of which was avouched handsomely by every General in the field, was done without the direct cost of a penny to the National Treasury. The Government indeed made no charge against the E.F.C. for services performed by its staff, nor for labour employed under Government contract, nor for accommodation available in Government vessels, nor for any expense that could not be fastened upon as imposing an additional burden on public funds. Moreover, as we have seen, there was some initial borrowing of capital. But every penny was paid off, with interest. The soldier on active service was better cared for than he had ever been. The soldier at home enjoyed greater facilities for comfort at a small expense than ever before. Both obtained better value for their money than at any previous time. The country profited by the better service which the soldier was thus enabled to give, and obtained that better service without any greater outlay. No contractor was enriched at the cost either of the taxpayer or the soldier. In brief, no one was the poorer for the labours of the E.F.C., and only the King's sailors and soldiers of all branches were the richer.

This is a very significant and astonishing fact. How was it brought about?

First and foremost by the steady persistence of those officers—at first only a very few—who twenty years before had insisted that the co-operative principle was the right one for the canteen-service, and had built up, in the Canteen and Mess Co-operative Society, an organisation which was capable of extending that principle on the vast scale which has been sketched in the foregoing pages.

Secondly, by the conversion of the principal contracting firm, Messrs R. Dickeson & Co., under the guidance of Sir Alexander Prince, to the co-operative system, and by the staunch support which he afterwards gave it. The officers above alluded to worked better than they knew. They had not aspired to greater things than to improve the lot of the soldier. But they succeeded not in this object only, but in benefiting all branches of the King's fighting services, and in doing inestimable good to their country without cost to the National Treasury.

The war came, as must all things, to an end. By
July 1919 the work of the E.F.C. was done; its
business was wound up; and its task was taken
over by the Navy and Army Canteen Board. Then
the question arose, what should be done next? and
in March 1920 the Secretary of State for War
appointed an inter-departmental committee, under
the chairmanship of Sir Archibald Williamson, to
advise: "Whether the present system of Navy and
Army Canteen Board should be continued without
modification or whether (so far as the Army is
concerned) it should be brought under War Office
administration." The committee unanimously decided that canteens, or institutes, as it was now
decided to call them, for the three services should
be administered by a joint organisation styled the
Navy, Army and Air Force Institute.

Accordingly the existing Navy, Army and Air
Force Institute came into being on the 1st of
January 1921. But even so there was still hesitation on the part of the authorities; and yet another
committee, this time of the House of Commons,
with Sir Samuel Roberts for chairman, was set
down to advise as to the principle involved in the
existence of the N.A.A.F.I. It reported its opinion
as follows:

From the evidence that we have heard, we are con-
vinced that the maintenance of a permanent organisa-

tion of the kind is most desirable as a matter of policy, both because of the amenities which it affords to members of the forces and more particularly because it provides the nucleus of a service capable of immediate expansion on mobilisation.

THE CO-OPERATIVE PRINCIPLE
FINALLY ACCEPTED

Thus at last the co-operative principle was accepted as that which should govern the canteen-service. In 1863 canteens had been made the subject of contract, and for fifty years that system had been accumulating the steady pile of damnation which reached its climax in the "canteen scandals" of 1914. The co-operative principle had been initiated (as may be once more repeated) in 1894. Lord Grey's Committee had recommended its adoption in 1902, but in vain. Four more committees in 1914, 1916, 1920 and 1921 upheld it; and it is interesting to note how many committees are necessary to break down a system which has been abundantly proved to be vicious. But in truth it was not the committees but the astounding work of the E.F.C., itself the offspring of the Canteen and Mess Co-operative Society, which fairly compelled the formation of a similar permanent organisation for the fighting services, not only in time of peace, but, if fate should ordain it, also in time of war.

Before going further, we must deal with the accumulated profits of the Expeditionary Force Canteens which were nicknamed the "Canteen Millions." These were handed over to the Army Council and, in accordance with the provision of War Service Canteens (Disposal of Surplus) Act 1922, were allocated to an United Services Fund, administered under the direction of General, Lord Byng.

THE PRESENT N.A.A.F.I.

The Navy, Army and Air Force Institute, as at present constituted, is the fulfilment of the dream of the founders of the Canteen and Mess Co-operative Society, and is, in fact, their own child. It is in principle a co-operative trading business conducted by those services for those services, including both officers and men. In the conduct of that business its revenue is for the three services and for them only. It is independent, in time of peace, of all official control. Every officer and man is *ipso facto* a participator in its benefits, and there are no other shareholders.

Its constitution consists of:

(1) A Council composed of four serving officers from each of the three services.

(2) A Board of Management, composed of three civilian business men, with a representative from each service.

(3) A General Manager.

It may be added here that the present General Manager[1] was in the service of the Canteen and Mess Co-operative Society thirty-three years ago, and was General Manager of the E.F.C. from the beginning to the end. Many of the important members of his staff came also from the Canteen and Mess Co-operative Society, so that there is no fear of their misunderstanding co-operative principles. He is also fortunate enough still to retain many of the most experienced employees formerly in the service of Messrs R. Dickeson & Co. He is thus well served both in principle and in practice.

The general policy of the N.A.A.F.I. is to afford facilities to its members of all three services to purchase commodities of high quality at prices competitive with those of "multiple" shops. This it is able to do through the vast scale of its purchases.

The revenue belongs to the three services, and is returned to them monthly in the form of rebates upon the receipts from the permanent institutes. The standard rate payable is 8 per cent., and to this is added a variable rebate, dependent on the trade results of the year, which in 1926 was 2 per cent. and in 1927 $2\frac{1}{2}$ per cent. The average monthly rebate per man in mess was in 1913, under the old contractors' system, 3s. 2d.; in 1926, under the N.A.A.F.I. it was 4s. 1½d.—a difference of over 25 per cent.

1 F. Benson.

At the time of writing, discount on cash purchases is allowed, at the rate of a penny in tenpence, to those entitled to draw discount instead of rebate. Discount on credit accounts is, to individuals, at the rate of a half-penny in tenpence, and of two shillings in the pound in respect of purchases by officers' and serjeants' messes. In the case of those who keep deposit-accounts the purchasing power of the amount deposited is increased by 10 per cent.

It is very obvious that contractors, who want profit for themselves, could offer no such terms.

Another object for the outlay of profit is the fitting out of Garrison and Regimental Institutes, so as to convert them into really attractive social clubs. Large sums have already been spent in refurnishing, and the standard thus raised will not be allowed to fall. Moreover, true to the traditions of the E.F.C., the N.A.A.F.I. provides parties of entertainers, which go the tour of the United Kingdom and give free entertainments for institutes, thus making those institutes more and more of a home for the soldier.

Furthermore, the N.A.A.F.I. looks as carefully to the well-being of the smallest as of the largest units. Before it came into existence, there was always, as has been told, a difficulty in finding contractors who would take over the canteens of small outlying detachments. Such little businesses did not pay; and the contractor, the essence of whose undertakings was his own profit, made what he could out of them by selling bad goods at high prices. But the N.A.A.F.I., working not for its own profit, sells goods of the same quality both to the largest and the smallest units.

THE FUTURE OF THE N.A.A.F.I.

To the present writer, who has followed the life of the British soldier closely through the centuries, the establishment of the N.A.A.F.I. presents itself as, on the whole, the greatest benefit that has ever been conferred upon the Army. As an ordinary householder he greatly envies the officers, soldiers and their families who are privileged to take advantage of it. Had they any conception of what their predecessors had to put up with, they would cherish it to the utmost. But man is a suspicious animal, and it is probable that the N.A.A.F.I. is not yet so well appreciated as it might be. Moreover, there is always a lingering apprehension in the soldier's mind—too well justified by past history—that his employer, the State, is always trying to get the better of him. Hence there remains the tendency, in case of any little failure or disappointment (for the institution which never was guilty of failure has never yet existed in this world), to blame some vague person or persons who are supposed to be at their old nefarious

75

work. In brief, the N.A.A.F.I. suffers still for the sins of Kit Ross, her predecessors and her successors.

But sailors and soldiers must rise above this prejudice. They must realise that the N.A.A.F.I. is not a force imposed upon them by external authority. It is their own Institute, built up by themselves for their own benefit. If they can improve it, they can do so; but the way to improvement is not by purposeless grumbling, but by practical suggestion. Above all they should bear in mind that the more heartily they support it, the greater its business will be, and the cheaper they will obtain their goods. It is *their* Institute, let it again be repeated, their very own; and the more they buy of it, the more will be returned to them.

As to those who are charged with the conduct of this vast business from the highest to the lowest, the writer can only envy them their proud position. He remembers the very beginning of the canteen-reforms in 1894 (having helped to count the coppers in the 17th Lancers' canteen-till) and the foundation of the Canteen and Mess Society. He knew all three of the principal founders—now long since dead—and was in the confidence not only of his brother but of that most accomplished physician and most lovable of men, Herbert Ramsay. He knew all their hopes and fears for the

Society, and, now that their dreams are realised, he stands amazed. Perhaps, having watched the growth of the Canteen and Mess Society from its birth to its development into the N.A.A.F.I., he can understand better than some others that it is, in modern slang, a very, very big thing.

But there is as hard work before it as behind it. Difficulties are never so great as at the moment of success. "There was," say the compilers of the prayer-book, "never anything by the wit of man so well devised or so sure established, which in continuance of time hath not been corrupted." It is not only for the staff of the Institute but for every officer and man to look to it that "the continuance of time" shall be long before corruption— not merely financial but moral, not merely through deliberate action but through apathy, carelessness or neglect—shall overtake the N.A.A.F.I. Those who are entrusted with its management from highest to lowest, have indeed a proud position, but they have also a stupendous responsibility not only to the three services of the present and future, but to thousands of earnest workers, both humble and exalted, in the past.

The N.A.A.F.I. is the flower of a plant which has been tended and nurtured by generations of British officers—almost entirely regimental—since the days of Cromwell. It has been a plant of slow growth, which has been blighted and thrown back

77

again and again, sometimes by misfortune, often by rascality, most often of all by stupidity, official and unofficial, political and military, individual and corporate. The story of the E.F.C., which represents the culmination of the efforts of those workers of the past, and of them who have taken over their task from them at present, should be not only known but a source of pride to every employee of the N.A.A.F.I. Nor, indeed, should any British officer be ignorant of it, for it is the creation of his own brethren for the welfare of all ranks of Navy, Army and Air Force.

Other men, whom we rightly honour, led the British soldier to ultimate victory in the Great War; but the E.F.C. was always behind them, keeping the soldier's heart up, physically and morally, for four long years in every part of the world and in the face of most formidable difficulties. This is the tradition which should inspire every one of the seven thousand men and women who now make up the staff of the N.A.A.F.I. It is their duty, first, to look to the welfare of the officers and men and of their families in time of peace, so that they may be always fit and happy and cheerful while learning and doing their work. Then, if war should come (and wars will not cease until men and women become angels), it is their lofty privilege to accompany the fighters into the field, and help to maintain their moral and physical force.

And they will follow them, not as the old contractors followed armies, to make money out of them—to stick to them as long as there was profit to be made, and to run away as soon as things looked unpleasant. Rather will they cling closely to them as friends and supporters, as they did faithfully from 1915 to 1918, undismayed by difficulty and undaunted by death, from sheer pride in their high calling, and from that zeal for the British soldier which is the grandest service that they can tender to their country.

They are now an essential part of the British fighting forces—let them never forget that—and their great tradition, handed down from the E.F.C., is to serve them that serve—to be all things to all fighting men.

Printed in the United States
By Bookmasters